CONTENTS

Practice

(A) Listen and write the letter. 05   **(B) Listen and repeat.** 06

| May I take your order? | Yes, please. I'd like a beef steak. |

1 a beef steak ☐

2 french fries ☐

3 noodles ☐

4 pancakes ☐

| How's your ice cream? | It's sweet. |

5 ice cream / sweet ☐

6 lemonade / sour ☐

7 cheese pizza / salty ☐

8 fried rice / spicy ☐

Listen & Talk

Ⓐ Listen and choose. 🎧 07

Ⓑ Check and say.

May I take your order?

Yes, please. I'd like _____.

pancakes

a cheese pizza

ice cream

Write & Talk

A Write, listen, and read. 08

Dad: Do you _____ some more salad?

Chris: Yes, _____.

Dad: _____ the fried rice?

Chris: It's _____, but it's delicious.

Dad: Do you want some _____?

Chris: No, thanks. I'm _____.

| full | spicy | How's | please | want | more |

B Look and write. Then ask and answer.

1 A: How's your _____?   B: It's _____.

2 A: How's your _____?   B: It's _____.

3 A: How's your _____?   B: It's _____.

juice	salty
chicken	spicy
fish	sour

Reading

What's your favorite dessert?

Crepes are my favorite dessert.

They are pancakes from France.

I like fruit crepes.

They are sweet and fresh.

I like to eat gelato.

Gelato is ice cream from Italy.

Lemon gelato is my favorite.

It is sweet and sour. It is delicious!

Try some. You will like it.

(B) **Choose or write.**

1 What is a crepe?

   ⓐ It's ice cream.   **ⓑ** It's a pancake.   **ⓒ** It's a donut.

2 Where is gelato from?

   ⓐ It's from Italy.   **ⓑ** It's from France.   **ⓒ** It's from China.

3 How's the lemon geleto? ⋯▸ It's _____ and _____.

Build Up

A Listen and repeat.  🎧 10

Do you want some **water**? - Yes, please.

Do you want some **noodles**? - No, thanks.

Do you want some **more chicken**? - Yes, please.

B Write and circle.

1
A: Do you want some _____?
B: (Yes, please. / No, thanks.)

| cookies |
| juice |
| bread |
| sandwiches |
| grapes |

2
A: Do you _____?
B: (Yes, please. / No, thanks.)

3
A: Do you _____ more _____?
B: (Yes, please. / No, thanks.)

4
A: Do _____ more _____?
B: (Yes, please. / No, thanks.)

5
A: Do _____ more _____?
B: (Yes, please. / No, thanks.)

Check-Up

A Listen and check. 🎧 11

1

2

3

4

B Listen and choose. 🎧 12

1

ⓐ ⓑ ⓒ

2

ⓐ ⓑ ⓒ

3

ⓐ ⓑ ⓒ

4

ⓐ ⓑ ⓒ

C Listen and circle T or F. 🎧 13

1 Tom wants a cheese burger. (T / F)

2 The chicken is sweet and salty. (T / F)

D Look and write.

1

A: May I take your _____?

B: Yes, please. I'd like _____.

2

A: _____ your lemonade?

B: It's _____.

3

A: Do you want _____ more _____?

B: _____ I'm full.

E Write and say.

1

A: May I take your order?

B: _____

2

A: How's your beef steak?

B: _____

These Glasses Look Funny

Mini Talk Look and listen. ▶ 🎧16

Oh, they look funny.

Dad, look at these glasses.

May I buy these glasses?

Sure.

I like them.

Listen and check.

1 T☐ F☐   2 T☐ F☐

Practice

| Look at this book. | It looks interesting. |
| Look at these jeans. | They look cool. |

1 book / interesting ☐

2 jeans / cool ☐

3 dress / beautiful ☐

4 glasses / funny ☐

5 mask / scary ☐

6
$$(3.5 - 1\frac{5}{6}) \times \frac{12}{17} = ?$$
quiz / difficult ☐

7 puzzle / easy ☐

8 fruits / fresh ☐

Unit 2 **11**

Listen & Talk

(A) Listen and match. 🎧 20

1
 •

a  •

• difficult

2
 •

b 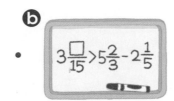 •

• interesting

3
 •

c  •

• scary

4
 •

d  •

• fresh

5
 •

e  •

• beautiful

This _____ looks _____.

These _____ look _____.

YOUR TURN (B) Check and say.

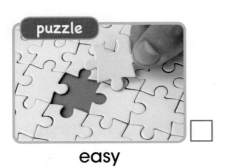
puzzle

easy

jeans

cool

dolls

funny

Write & Talk

A Write, listen, and read. 🎧21

Mom: Look at this shirt. It _____ cute.

Paul: I don't like yellow.

Mom: How about this _____?

Paul: Oh, it looks _____. I like it.

Mom: _____ is it?

Clerk: It's _____ dollars.

| T-shirt | looks | How much | twenty | cool |

B Look and write. Then say.

| 1 | 2 | 3 | 4 |
| movie | dog | shoes | fruits |

1 Look at this _____. It looks _____.

2 Look at _____. _____

3 Look at these _____. They look _____.

4 Look at _____. _____

| fresh |
| cute |
| funny |
| interesting |

Reading

 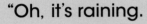
"Oh, it's raining.

That's Terry's house."

Ann goes into the house.

Some soup and bread are on the table.

They look delicious.

Some fruits are in the basket.

They look fresh.

Terry is sleeping in his bed.

"You look cute.

Have a good dream."

B Circle or write.

1   The soup and bread look delicious.   (T / F)

2   Terry is eating some fruits.   (T / F)

3   He looks _____.

14

Build Up

A Listen and repeat. 🎧 23

look, looks

The boy **looks** happy. The cat **looks** cute. These fruits **look** fresh.

B Look and write.

beautiful	funny	interesting	delicious	sleepy

1 This game looks _____.

2 These birds _____.

3 The man _____.

4 The boy _____.

5 These cupcakes _____.

Check-Up

Ⓐ Listen and choose. 🎧24

1
 ⓐ   ⓑ

2
ⓐ    ⓑ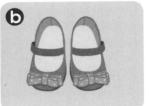

3
ⓐ 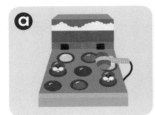   ⓑ

4
ⓐ    ⓑ

Ⓑ Listen and number. 🎧25

 ☐

 ☐

 ☐

 ☐

Ⓒ Listen and circle T or F. 🎧26

1   The game looks difficult.   (T / F)

2   The red dress looks beautiful.   (T / F)

D Look, circle, and write.

1

scary

A: Look at (this / these) _____.

B: (It / They) looks _____.

2

interesting

A: Look at (this / these) _____.

B: (It / They) _____.

3

fresh

A: Look at (this / these) _____.

B: (It / They) _____.

E Write and say.

1

A: Look at this monkey.

B: _____

2

A: _____

B: They look cool.

Review ①

Ⓐ Look and write.

> It looks scary. May I take your order?
>
> How's your cookie? I'd like a hamburger.

Yes, please.

I'd like pancakes and cookies.

Look at my hamburger.

My pancakes look cute.

It's sweet.

B Read and number.

1 A: May I take your order?

B: Yes, please.

I'd like a beef steak.

2 A: Do you want some noodles?

B: Yes, please.

3 A: How's your fried rice?

B: It's salty.

C Match and write.

1

A: Look at this dress.

B: _____

2

A: Look at this puzzle.

B: _____

3

A: Look at these glasses.

B: _____

They look funny.   It looks easy.   It looks beautiful.

How Much Are the Jeans?

Mini Talk Look and listen.

May I help you?

Yes, please.
How much are the jeans?

They're twenty dollars.

What size do you want?

I want a small, please.

CHECK 30

1 How much are the jeans?   a ☐ b ☐
2 What size does the boy want?   a ☐ b ☐

20

Practice

A Listen and write the letter. 🎧 31   **B** Listen and repeat. 🎧 32

How much are the jeans? : They're thirty dollars.

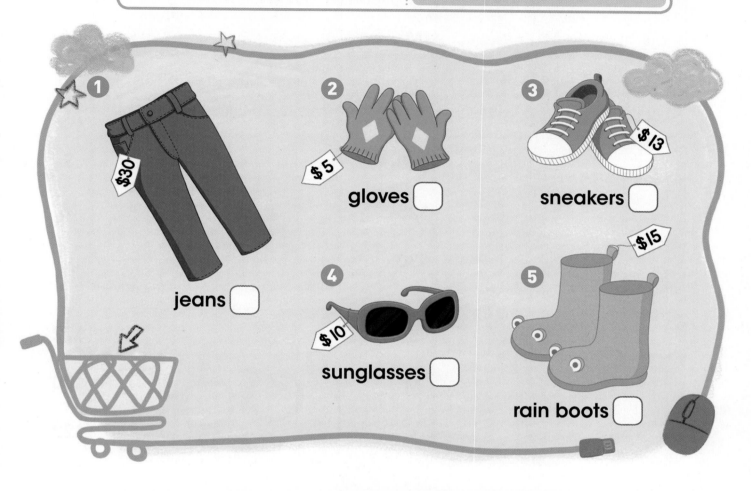

1 $30 — jeans ☐

2 $5 — gloves ☐

3 $13 — sneakers ☐

4 $10 — sunglasses ☐

5 $15 — rain boots ☐

What size do you want? : I want a small, please.

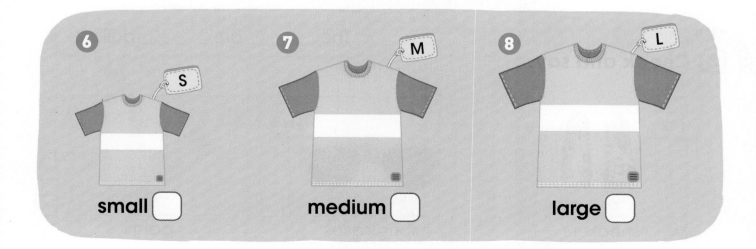

6 S — small ☐

7 M — medium ☐

8 L — large ☐

Listen & Talk

A Listen, number, and circle. 🎧 33

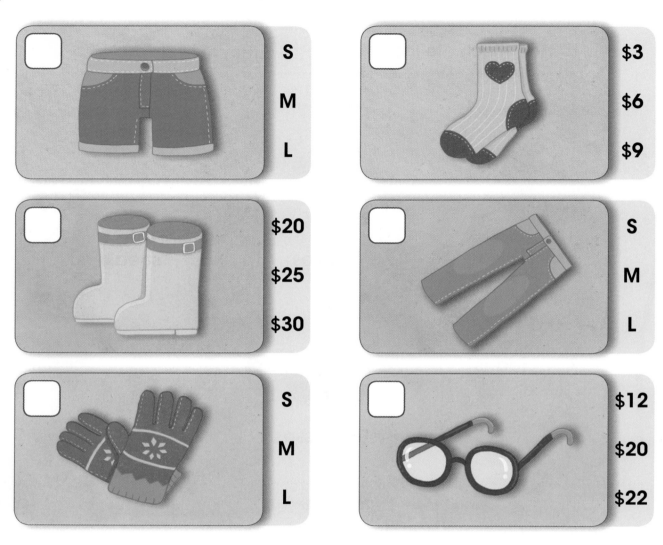

YOUR TURN

B Check and say.

The _____ are _____ dollars.

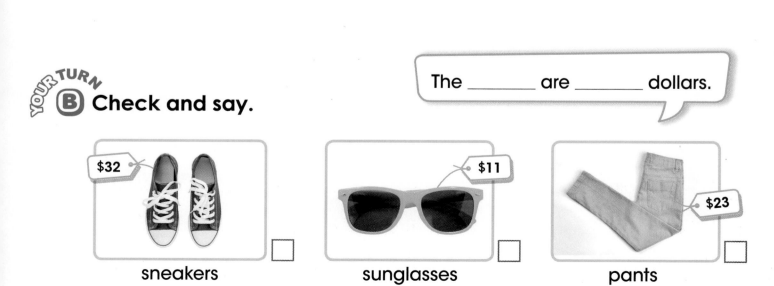

sneakers

sunglasses

pants

Write & Talk

A Write, listen, and read. 🎧34

Fred: I'm looking for _____.

Clerk: What _____ do you want?

Fred: I _____ blue, please.

Clerk: How about these?

Fred: They _____ nice.

　　　Can I _____ them on?

Clerk: Sure.

| try | want | gloves | color | look |

B Look and write. Then ask and answer.

1　A: _____ do you want?　B: I want _____.

2　A: What color _____?　B: I _____.

3　A: _____ do you want?　B: I want a _____.

4　A: What size _____?　B: I _____.

medium
large
blue
pink

Reading

Listen and read.

I want those sneakers.

They are red and white.

They look cool.

I'll buy them.

How much are they?

They're twenty two dollars.

But I have only twenty in my wallet.

Oh, they're on sale. They're twenty dollars.

I'm lucky.

B Circle or write.

1 The boy wants new sneakers.   (T / F)

2 The sneakers are red and blue.   (T / F)

3 How much are the sneakers?

   ⋯▸ They're _____ dollars.

Build Up

A Listen and repeat. 🎧 36

What color ~?

 What color do you want?   - I want pink.

 What size do you want?   - I want a medium.

 What sport do you like?   - I like baseball.

B Write and circle.

color
sport
size
animal
food

1

A: _____ do you want?

B: I want a (small / large).

2

A: _____ do you want?

B: I want (blue / red).

3

A: _____ do you want?

B: I want (spaghetti / fried rice).

4

A: _____ do you like?

B: I like (baseball / soccer).

5

A: _____ do you like?

B: I like (monkeys / pandas).

Check-Up

A Listen and number. 37

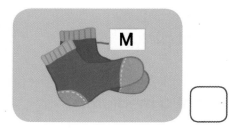

B Listen and choose. 38

1  ⓐ ⓑ

2  ⓐ ⓑ

3 ⓐ ⓑ

4  ⓐ ⓑ

C Listen and choose. 39

1 What size does the boy want?

ⓐ He wants a small. ⓑ He wants a medium. ⓒ He wants a large.

2 How much are the jeans?

ⓐ They're five dollars. ⓑ They're fifteen dollars. ⓒ They're fifty dollars.

D Look and write.

1

A: _____ _____ are the gloves?

B: They're _____ dollars.

2

A: _____ _____ do you want?

B: I want a _____, please.

3

A: _____ _____ do you want?

B: I want _____.

E Write and say.

1

A: How much are the sunglasses?

B: _____

2

A: What size do you want?

B: _____

I Went to the Water Park

Mini Talk Look and listen.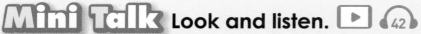

What did you do during the vacation?

I joined the English camp. How about you?

I went to the water park.

Sounds fun.

CHECK 43

Listen and check.

1 T ☐ F ☐   2 T ☐ F ☐

Practice

(A) Listen and write the letter. 🎧44   **(B)** Listen and repeat. 🎧45

What did you do during the vacation?   I went camping.

during the vacation

1. went camping ☐
2. went to the water park ☐
3. read many books ☐
4. swam at the beach ☐

last weekend

5. made a model plane ☐
6. ate Mexican food ☐
7. saw a parade ☐
8. flew a drone ☐

Listen & Talk

(A) Listen and write T or F. 🎧 46

1.

2.

3.

4.

5.

6.

YOUR TURN
(B) Check and say.

I _____ last weekend.

went camping

saw a parade

went to the zoo

30

Write & Talk

A Write, listen, and read. 🎧 47

Ben: What did you do _____?

Kate: I _____ to the zoo.

Ben: What did you see _____?

Kate: I _____ an animal parade.

I _____ a bird show, too.

Ben: Sounds fun.

| watched | yesterday | there | went | saw |

B Match and write. Then ask and answer.

What did you do yesterday?

① went

② made

③ read

④ flew

comic books   camping   a model car   a drone

1 I _____ with friends.   2 I _____ with my dad.

3 I _____ at home.   4 I _____ at the park.

Reading

Brian went to the beach last weekend.

He went there with Tim.

They played together.

They swam at the beach.

They made a sand castle, too.

It was fun.

Lunch was delicious.

They ate hot dogs and french fries.

They had a great time.

Ⓑ Choose or write.

1   Brian _____ last weekend.

ⓐ went to the beach   ⓑ went fishing   ⓒ visited his friend

2   He _____ with Tim.

ⓐ made lunch   ⓑ made a sand castle   ⓒ drew a picture

3   What did they eat for lunch? ⟶ They _____.

Build Up

A Listen and repeat. 49

			made
make – made	draw – drew	fly – flew	ride – rode
swim – swam	see – saw	read – read	have – had

B Change and write.

ride	make	draw	fly	have

1

I _____ a robot last Monday.

2

We _____ a picnic last weekend.

3

They _____ kites yesterday.

4

He _____ many pictures during the vacation.

5

We _____ bikes yesterday.

Check-Up

A Listen and check. 🎧50

1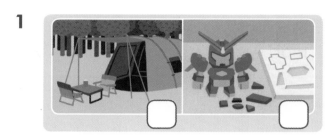

2

3

4

B Listen and choose. 🎧51

1 ⓐ ⓑ

2 ⓐ ⓑ

3 ⓐ ⓑ

4 ⓐ ⓑ

C Listen and match. 🎧52

1

Kevin •

2

Lily •

• had a picnic •

• read comic books •

• made a robot •

• yesterday.

• last weekend.

34

D Look and write.

1

A: _____ _____ you do last weekend?

B: I _____ a parade. It was great.

2

A: What _____ you do yesterday?

B: I _____ Mexican food.
It was delicious.

3

I _____ camping _____ the vacation.

I _____ a good time.

E Write and say.

1

A: What did you do during the vacation?

B: _____

2

A: What did you do last weekend?

B: _____
It was fun.

A Look and write.

> How much are the sunglasses?
> Can I try them on?
>
> What did you do last weekend?
> I had a good time there.

B Read and write T or F.

1  **$15**

A: How much are these sneakers?

B: They're fifteen dollars.

☐

2

A: I'm looking for boots.

B: What color do you want?

A: I want blue.

☐

3  **M**

A: I like this cap.

B: What size do you want?

A: I want a medium, please.

☐

C Look and write.

❶

1 A: What did you do during the vacation?

B: _____

❷

2 A: What did she do last weekend?

B: _____

❸

3 A: What did he do yesterday?

B: _____

I made a model plane.   He went camping.   She saw a parade.

Mini Talk Look and listen. ▶ 🎧 55

What did you do yesterday?

I went to the flower festival. It was fantastic.

Did you take pictures?

Yes, I did. Look.

CHECK 56

1 What did the girl do yesterday?   a ☐   b ☐
2 Did she take pictures?   a ☐   b ☐

Practice

A Listen and write the letter. 🎧 57   **B** Listen and repeat. 🎧 58

Did you **have lunch**?   Yes, I did.
No, I didn't.

have lunch ☐

see dolphins ☐

take a shower ☐

get a haircut ☐

buy the tickets ☐

water the plants ☐

bring your swimsuit ☐

do your homework ☐

Listen & Talk

(A) Listen, number, and circle. 🎧59

(B) Check and say.

Did you _____?

Yes, I did. / No, I didn't.

see dolphins

do your homework

bring your swimsuit

Write & Talk

Write, listen, and read. 🎧 60

Jane: You look _____.

_____ you get a haircut today?

Dick: Yes, I did. _____ was your day?

Jane: It was good. I _____ the Sea Park.

Dick: Did you _____ dolphins there?

Jane: Yes, I did. I _____ with the dolphins.

| How | nice | see | Did | visited | played |

B **Look and write. Then ask and answer.**

1 A: Did you _____?   B: _____, _____.

2 A: _____ you _____?   B: _____, _____.

3 A: _____?   B: _____, _____.

| have lunch | clean your room | water the flowers |

Reading

A **Listen and read.** 🎧61

Dear Sam,

Did you have a good day?

I had a great day.

I went to the circus.

I saw a big elephant there.

He played with a big ball.

I saw a cute bear, too.

She rode a bike very well.

The circus was fantastic.

What did you do today?

From John

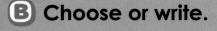

B **Choose or write.**

1 What did John do today?
   ⓐ He watched a magic show.   ⓑ He went to the circus.

2 Did he see an elephant?
   ⓐ Yes, he did.   ⓑ No, he didn't.

3 How was the circus? ⋯› It _____ .

Build Up

Ⓐ Listen and repeat. 🎧62

Did you ~?

Did you fly a kite?
Yes, I did. / No, I didn't.

Did she water the plants?
Yes, she did. / No, she didn't.

Ⓑ Look and write.

bring	do	swim	make	have

1 ✗

A: Did you _____ your homework?

B: No, I _____.

2 ○

A: _____ at the beach?

B: Yes, I _____.

3 ✗

A: _____ her swimsuit?

B: No, she _____.

4 ○

A: _____ dinner today?

B: Yes, she _____.

5 ✗

A: _____ a model plane?

B: No, he _____.

Check-Up

(A) Listen, number, and match. 🎧 63

Yes, I did.

No, I didn't.

(B) Listen and write T or F. 🎧 64

1

2

3

4

(C) Listen and choose. 🎧 65

1 Denny didn't _____.

   ⓐ watch a movie   ⓑ do his homework   ⓒ have dinner

2 Lucy didn't _____.

   ⓐ play outside   ⓑ bring her umbrella   ⓒ buy the tickets

44

D Look and write.

1

A: Did you _____ your homework?

B: _____, _____.

2

A: Did you _____ lunch?

B: _____, _____. I'm hungry.

3

A: _____ she _____ a haircut?

B: _____, _____.

E Write and say.

1

A: _____

B: Yes, I did.

2

A: _____

B: No, I didn't.

Practice

A Listen and write the letter. 🎧 70   **B** Listen and repeat. 🎧 71

What's in the **bedroom**?

There is **a** closet.

There are **two** beds.

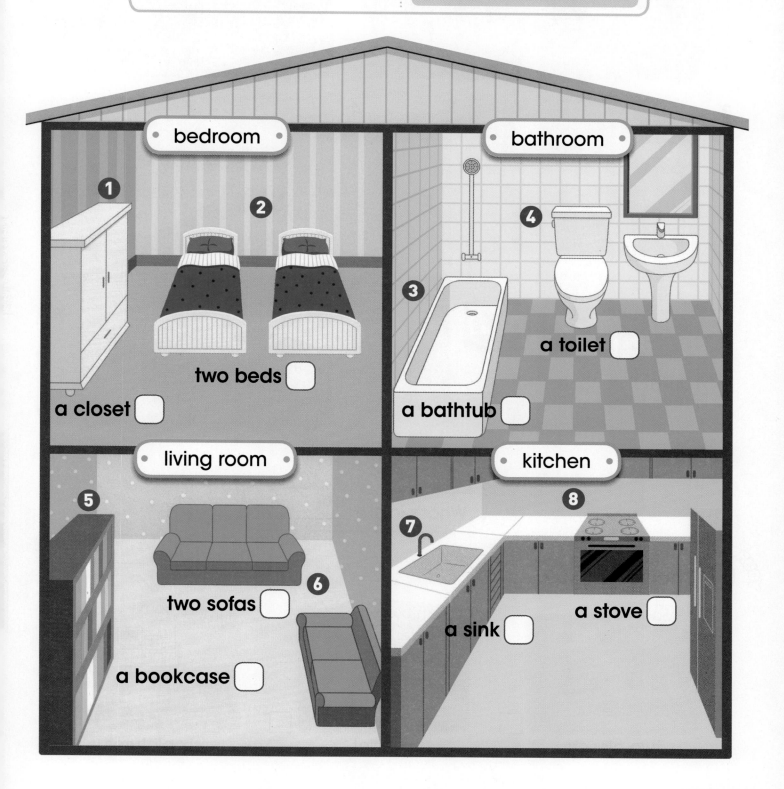

bedroom

1

2

two beds ☐

a closet ☐

bathroom

4

3

a toilet ☐

a bathtub ☐

living room

5

6

two sofas ☐

a bookcase ☐

kitchen

8

7

a sink ☐

a stove ☐

Listen & Talk

A Listen and circle T or F. 🎧72

1
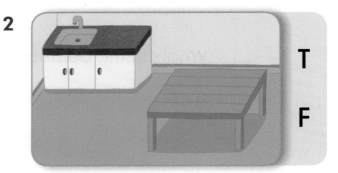
T
F

2

T
F

3

T
F

4

T
F

5
T
F

6

T
F

What's in the _____?

There is/are _____.

YOUR TURN
B Check and say.

bedroom

two closets

bathroom

a toilet

living room

six pictures

Write & Talk

A Write, listen, and read. 🎧 73

Sue: There are pictures _____.

Dan: My mom likes drawing _____.

Sue: There are _____.

Does she _____ reading books, too?

Dan: Yes, but the books are mine.

You can _____ them.

| pictures | borrow | many books | like | on the wall |

B Look and write. Then say.

There is ....

There are ....

| a closet | many toys |
| a book | two pictures |

1 _____ in the room. 2 _____ on the wall.

3 _____ on the bed. 4 _____ in the box.

Reading

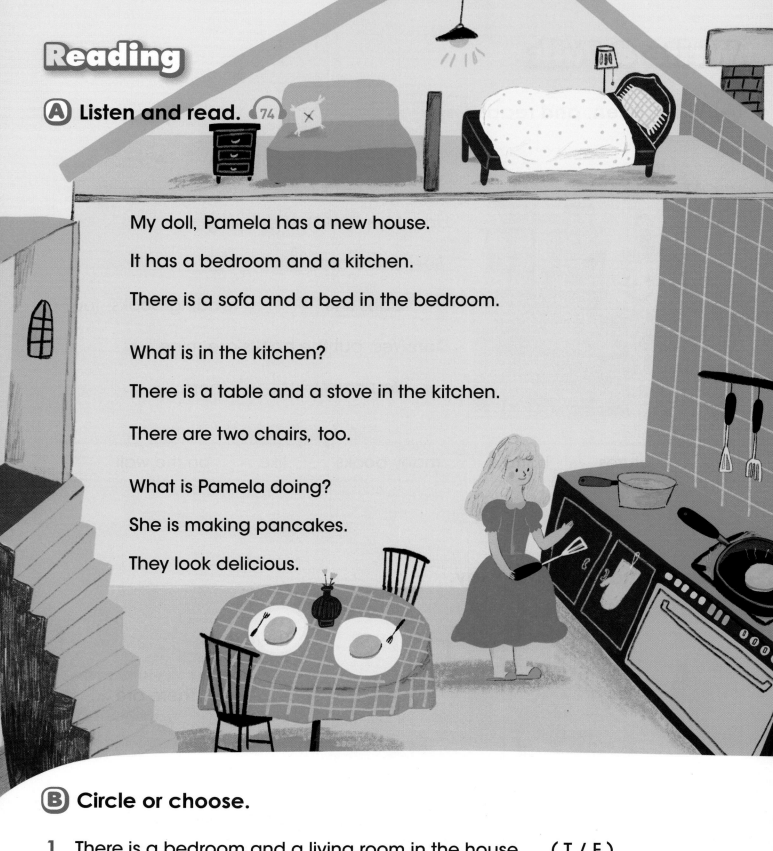

My doll, Pamela has a new house.

It has a bedroom and a kitchen.

There is a sofa and a bed in the bedroom.

What is in the kitchen?

There is a table and a stove in the kitchen.

There are two chairs, too.

What is Pamela doing?

She is making pancakes.

They look delicious.

Ⓑ **Circle or choose.**

1 There is a bedroom and a living room in the house.   (T / F)

2 There is a sofa and a bed in the bedroom.   (T / F)

3 What's in the kitchen?

   ⓐ There is a sink.　　　ⓑ There are chairs.　　　ⓒ There are pictures.

Build Up

A Listen and repeat.  🎧 75

> There is/are ~.

There is a sofa in the living room.
There are two cats on the sofa.
There is a lamp next to the sofa.
There are socks under the table.

B Look and write.

| a pot | pictures | some books | a cap | a toilet |

1

There _____ in the bathroom.

2

_____ next to the piano.

3

_____ on the desk.

4

_____ on the wall.

5

_____ under the bed.

Ⓐ Listen and number. 🎧76

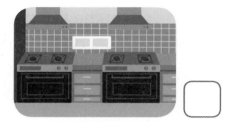

Ⓑ Listen and choose. 🎧77

1 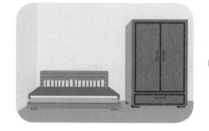 ⓐ ⓑ

2  ⓐ ⓑ

3 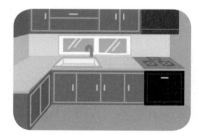 ⓐ ⓑ

4  ⓐ ⓑ

Ⓒ Listen and circle T or F. 🎧78

1   There are sandwiches on the table.   (T / F)

2   There are two computers in the bedroom.   (T / F)

D Look and write.

1

A: What's in the _____?

B: There is _____ and a stove.

2

A: What's in the _____?

B: There _____ a closet.

There _____ two beds, too.

3

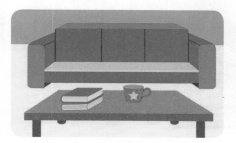

_____ a sofa in the living room.

_____ two books _____ the table.

E Write and say.

1

A: What's in the bathroom?

B: _____

2

A: What's in the living room?

B: _____

Review 3

A Look and write.

What's in the bedroom?	There is a big bathtub.
There is a bedroom and a bathroom.	Did you bring your homework?

Ⓑ Match and check.

1

Did she get a haircut?

☐ Yes, she did. ☐ No, she didn't.

2

Did you take a shower?

☐ Yes, I did. ☐ No, I didn't.

3

Did he see dolphins there?

☐ Yes, he did. ☐ No, he didn't.

Ⓒ Look and write the letter.

1 What's in the bedroom? _____

2 What's in the bathroom? _____

3 What's in the kitchen? _____, _____

4 What's in the living room? _____, _____

ⓐ There is a bathtub. ⓑ There is a sofa. ⓒ There are two stoves.

ⓓ There are three closets. ⓔ There is a sink. ⓕ There are two bookcases.

I Want to Play Outside

Mini Talk Look and listen. 🎬 🎧81

I'm so bored.

What do you want to do, Tina?

I want to play outside.

But I'm reading a comic book now. I have a good idea.

CHECK 82

1 What does Tina want to do? a ☐ b ☐
2 What is the boy doing? a ☐ b ☐

Practice

A Listen and write the letter. 83

B Listen and repeat. 84

What do you want to do? | I want to go to the sea.

1. go to the sea
2. travel to Paris
3. climb the mountain
4. catch fireflies
5. buy new clothes
6. read comic books
7. listen to music
8. ride a scooter

Listen & Talk

(A) Listen and choose. 🎧 85

1
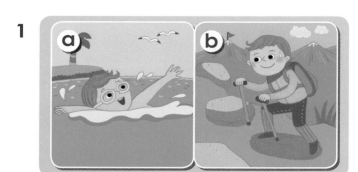

2

3

4

5

6

(B) Check and say.

What do you want to do?

I want to _____.

catch fireflies

go to the sea

ride a scooter

58

Write & Talk

(A) Write, listen, and read. 🎧 86

Dad: What do you _____ to do today?

Dona: I want _____. I'm tired.

But I'm hungry.

Dad: Okay. Then I'll _____ for you.

_____ do you want to eat?

Dona: I want _____ spaghetti.

Dad: Good. That's easy.

| want | to eat | to sleep | cook | What |

What does he/she want to do?

(B) Look and write. Then ask and answer.

1 She wants to _____.　2 He _____.

3 She _____.　4 He _____.

| sing songs | watch movies | go shopping | play with friends |

Reading

A Listen and read.  87

The school concert is this Friday.

My friends and I will play music.

Sally wants to play the piano.

Ron wants to play the guitar.

Tom wants to play the drums.

"Kate, what will you do?"

I can't play the piano or the guitar.

I don't like to play the drums.

But I like to sing.

I want to sing songs.

B Circle or choose.

1   The school concert is this Friday.   (T / F)

2   Ron wants to play the piano.   (T / F)

3   Kate wants to _____.

   ⓐ play the drums   ⓑ play the guitar   ⓒ sing songs

Build Up

Ⓐ Listen and repeat. 🎧 88

don't want to, want to

I **don't want to** read books.
I **want to** sleep.

I **don't like to** climb the mountain.
I **like to** swim at the beach.

Ⓑ Look and write.

1

I don't want _____ a bike.

I want _____ a scooter.

2

I _____ like _____ math.

I like _____ sports.

3

I _____ want _____ the mountain.

I want _____ the museum.

4

I _____ like _____ the piano.

I _____ computer games.

5

I _____ want _____ home.

I _____ outside.

climb
stay
watch
ride
play
visit
study

Check-Up

A Listen and number. 🎧89

 ☐

 ☐

 ☐

 ☐

B Listen and choose. 🎧90

1  ⓐ ⓑ

2  ⓐ ⓑ

3  ⓐ ⓑ

4  ⓐ ⓑ

C Listen and circle. 🎧91

1 The boy wants to (catch fireflies / go hiking).

2 The girl wants to (climb the mountain / go to the sea).

D Look and write.

1 A: What _____ you want to do?

 B: I want _____ to China.

2 A: What _____ you want to buy?

 B: I _____ new sneakers.

3 A: What _____ he want to do?

 B: He _____ a scooter.

4 A: What _____ she want to do?

 B: She _____ to music.

E Write and say.

1

A: What do you want to do?

B: _____

2

A: What do you want to do?

B: _____

What Do You Want to Be?

Mini Talk Look and listen. ▶ 🎧94

I want to be a famous singer. I like singing.

Sounds great!

What do you want to be, James?

I want to be a vet. I want to help animals.

⊙ CHECK 95

1 Does the girl like singing? a ☐ b ☐
2 What does James want to be? a ☐ b ☐

Practice

A Listen and write the letter. 96

B Listen and repeat. 97

What do you want to be?

I want to be a designer.
I want to design clothes.

designer
1 design clothes ☐

writer
2 write stories ☐

teacher
3 teach children ☐

movie director
4 make movies ☐

vet
5 help animals ☐

pilot
6 fly planes ☐

photographer
7 take great pictures ☐

traveler
8 travel around the world ☐

Listen & Talk

A Listen and match. 🎧98

1 •   • writer •   • ⓐ

2 •   • photographer •   • ⓑ

3 •   • movie director •   • ⓒ

4 •   • traveler •   • ⓓ

5 •   • designer •   • ⓔ

> What do you want to be?

> I want to be a _____.
>
> I want to _____.

YOUR TURN B Check and say.

pilot
fly planes ☐

teacher
teach children ☐

vet
help animals ☐

Write & Talk

A Write, listen, and read. 🎧99

Kelly: Do you like _____ cars?

Ted: Yes, I do. I want to be a _____.

How about you?

Kelly: I want to be a _____.

I want to travel _____.

Ted: Sounds great.

| around the world | to draw | traveler | car designer |

B Match and write. Then ask and answer.

What do you want to be?

1 pilot

2 police officer

3 cook

make delicious food   **fly planes**   **help people**

1 I want to _____. I want to _____.

2 I want _____. I want _____.

3 I _____. I _____.

Reading

Ⓐ Listen and read. 🎧 100

I like to watch movies.

I want to be a movie director.

I want to make science movies.

I will join the movie festival this summer.

FIFA WORLD CUP

Brad likes to play soccer.

He wants to be a soccer player.

He wants to win the World Cup.

He will join the soccer camp this vacation.

Ⓑ Circle or write.

1   The girl wants to make movies.   (T / F)

2   She will join the soccer camp this summer.   (T / F)

3   What does Brad want to be?

　　⟶ He wants to be a _____.

Build Up

A Listen and repeat. 🎧101

I want to be a doctor.
I want to help sick people.

He wants to be a writer.
He wants to write stories.

B Look and write.

1

I want to _____ a teacher.

I want to _____.

2

I want _____ a vet.

I want _____.

make robots
take good pictures
help animals
teach math
design clothes

3

He wants _____ a photographer.

He wants _____.

4

She wants _____ a designer.

She wants _____.

5

They _____ scientists.

They want _____.

Check-Up

(A) Listen and choose. 🎧102

1

ⓐ ⓑ ⓒ

2

ⓐ ⓑ ⓒ

3

ⓐ ⓑ ⓒ

4

ⓐ ⓑ ⓒ

(B) Listen and number. 🎧103

(C) Listen and choose. 🎧104

1 Jane wants to be a _____.

ⓐ photographer   ⓑ traveler   ⓒ teacher

2 Tony likes to _____.

ⓐ write stories   ⓑ make clothes   ⓒ make movies

D Look and write.

1

A: What do you want to be?

B: I want to _____ a _____.

I want _____.

2

A: What do you _____?

B: I want to be a _____.

I want _____.

3

He wants to be a _____.

He wants _____.

E Write and say.

1

A: What do you want to be?

B: _____

2

I want to be _____.

I want _____.

Ⓐ Look and write.

What do you want to be?	I want to fly planes.
I want to teach English.	Do you want to be a pilot?

They look cool!
_____

_____
_____

Yes, I do.

_____

I want to be a teacher.

What do you want to teach?

_____

B **Match and write the number.**

1 What do you want to do? • • He wants to buy new clothes.

2 What does she want to do? • • She wants to read comic books.

3 What does he want to do? • • I want to climb the mountain.

C **Read and write.**

1 I want to be a movie director.
   _____

2 She wants to be a writer.
   _____

3 I want to be a vet.
   _____

She wants to write stories.   I want to make movies.   I want to help animals.

Our Sunday Morning Breakfast  105

It was Sunday morning.

I made breakfast with Mom and Dad.

Mom made strawberry pancakes.

They looked delicious.

I love strawberries.

Dad made a vegetable salad.

It looked fresh.

But I don't like vegetables.

I made lemonade.

It was sweet and sour.

1 This story is about _____.

    ⓐ eating desserts   ⓑ making breakfast   ⓒ helping Mom and Dad

Comprehension

2 Mom made _____.

    ⓐ a vegetable salad   ⓑ strawberry pancakes   ⓒ lemonade

3 The vegetable salad looked _____.

    ⓐ delicious   ⓑ sour   ⓒ fresh

4 How was the lemonade?

    ⓐ It was salty.   ⓑ It was sweet and sour.   ⓒ It was sweet and spicy.

Writing Practice

What did you do last Sunday? ⋯⋯▸ I made breakfast.

1 What did you do during the vacation?

    ⋯⋯▸ I _____. (go to the water park)

2 What did you do last weekend?

    ⋯⋯▸ I _____. (read many books)

Thanks, Doctor

Dan is in the hospital.

He is sad.

He wants to go home.

He wants to eat Grandma's pie.

"Mom, did you bring Grandma's pie?"

"Sorry, I didn't."

"Dr. Jordan, can I go home today?"

"Sure. You are okay."

"Really? Thanks, Doctor."

"Dr. Jordan is nice.

 I want to be a nice doctor, too."

1 This story is about _____.

ⓐ Grandma's pie   ⓑ a good doctor   ⓒ a boy in the hospital

Comprehension

2 Where is Dan?

ⓐ He is in his bedroom.

ⓑ He is in his grandma's house.

ⓒ He is in the hospital.

3 Dan wants to _____.

ⓐ eat Grandma's pie   ⓑ be a teacher   ⓒ play outside

4 Dan can _____ today.

ⓐ go to the hospital   ⓑ go home   ⓒ visit his friend

Writing Practice

What does he want to be? ⟶ He wants to be a doctor.

1 What do you want to be?

⟶ I _____. (pilot)

2 What does she want to be?

⟶ She _____. (teacher)

• Present Simple

verb + -s / -es / -ies					
bake	bakes		have	has	
bring	brings		help	helps	
buy	buys		make	makes	
catch	catches		meet	meets	
clean	cleans		paint	paints	
come	comes		play	plays	
cry	cries		read	reads	
dance	dances		ride	rides	
do	does		run	runs	
draw	draws		study	studies	
drink	drinks		take	takes	
eat	eats		teach	teaches	
finish	finishes		walk	walks	
fly	flies		wash	washes	
go	goes		watch	watches	

Past Simple

Regular Verbs		
bake	baked	
clean	cleaned	
dance	danced	
help	helped	
join	joined	
learn	learned	
listen	listened	
look	looked	
practice	practiced	
plant	planted	
play	played	
visit	visited	
want	wanted	
wash	washed	
watch	watched	

Irregular Verbs		
am	was	
are	were	
do	did	
draw	drew	
eat	ate	
fly	flew	
go	went	
have	had	
is	was	
read	read	
ride	rode	
see	saw	
swim	swam	
take	took	
write	wrote	

Word List 4C

Unit 1 I'd Like a Chocolate Ice Cream Cone

beef steak _____

cheese pizza _____

french fries _____

fried rice _____

ice cream _____

lemonade _____

noodles _____

pancake _____

salad _____

salty _____

sour _____

spicy _____

sweet _____

Unit 2 These Glasses Look Funny

beautiful _____

cool _____

difficult _____

easy _____

fresh _____

fruit _____

funny _____

glasses _____

interesting _____

mask _____

puzzle _____

quiz _____

scary _____

Unit 3 How Much Are the Jeans?

color _____

gloves _____

large _____

medium _____

rain boots _____

sale _____

shorts _____

size _____

small _____

sneakers _____

socks _____

sunglasses _____

try ~ on _____

Unit 4 I Went to the Water Park

ate Mexican food _____

drew a picture _____

during the vacation _____

last weekend _____

flew a drone _____

had a picnic _____

made a model plane _____

read many books _____

rode a bike _____

saw a parade _____

swam at the beach _____

went camping _____

went to the water park _____

Unit 5 Did You Take Pictures?

bring your swimsuit _____
buy the tickets _____
clean your room _____
do your homework _____
fly a kite _____
get a haircut _____
have a good day _____
have lunch _____
make a model plane _____
see dolphins _____
take a shower _____
take pictures _____
water the plants _____

Unit 6 There Is a Nice Bed

bathroom _____
bathtub _____
bed _____
bedroom _____
bookcase _____
closet _____
kitchen _____
living room _____
sink _____
sofa _____
stove _____
toilet _____
wall _____

Unit 7 I Want to Play Outside

buy new clothes _____
catch fireflies _____
climb the mountain _____
cook food _____
have a good idea _____
go to the sea _____
listen to music _____
play music _____
play outside _____
play the piano _____
read comic books _____
ride a scooter _____
travel to Paris _____

Unit 8 What Do You Want to Be?

design clothes _____
designer _____
fly planes _____
help animals _____
help sick people _____
make delicious food _____
make movies _____
movie director _____
teach children _____
photographer _____
travel around the world _____
win the World Cup _____
write stories _____

Syllabus 4C

Unit 1 I'd Like a Chocolate Ice Cream Cone

Structures	Vocabulary			Grammar
• May I take your order?	beef steak	ice cream	sour	Do you want some ~?
Yes, please. I'd like a chocolate ice cream cone.	cheese pizza	juice	salty	
• How's the ice cream?	chicken	lemonade	spicy	
It's sweet.	french fries	noodles	sweet	
• Do you want some fried rice?	fried rice	pancake	full	
Yes, please. / No, thanks. I'm full.	fish	salad	delicious	

Unit 2 These Glasses Look Funny

Structures	Vocabulary			Grammar
• Look at this book.	beautiful	funny	glasses	look, looks
It looks interesting.	cool	interesting	jeans	
• Look at these glasses.	cute	scary	mask	
They look funny.	difficult	book	puzzle	
• This quiz looks easy.	easy	dress	quiz	
	fresh	fruit		**Reading**

Review 1

Unit 3 How Much Are the Jeans?

Structures	Vocabulary			Grammar
• May I help you? – Yes, please.	gloves	size	pink	What color ~?
• How much are the jeans?	jeans	small	red	
They're twenty dollars.	rain boots	medium	white	
• What size do you want?	sneakers	large	yellow	
I want a small, please.	sunglasses	color	try	
• What color do you want?	shorts	blue	sale	
I want blue, please.	socks	green		**Reading**

Unit 4 I Went to the Water Park

Structures	Vocabulary		Grammar
• What did you do during the vacation?	ate Mexican food	rode a bike	make - made
I joined the English camp.	drew a picture	saw a parade	
• How about you?	flew a drone	swam at the beach	
• What did you see there?	had a picnic	went camping	
I saw an animal parade.	made a model plane	went to the water park	
• Sounds fun(good, great).	read many books		**Reading**

Review 2

Unit 5 Did You Take Pictures?

Structures	Vocabulary		Grammar

•Did you(she) take pictures?
  Yes, I(she) did. /No, I(she) didn't.
•What did you do yesterday?
  I went to the flower festival.
	bring your swimsuit
	buy the tickets
	do your homework
	get a haircut
		have lunch
		see dolphins
		take a shower
		water the plants
			Did you ~?
			
			Reading

Unit 6 There Is a Nice Bed

Structures	Vocabulary			Grammar

• This is my new house.
• What's in the room?
  There is a nice bed.
  There are many books.
•There is a big TV in the living room.
	bathroom
	bedroom
	kitchen
	living room
	bathtub
	bed
		bookcase
		chair
		closet
		house
		lamp
		picture
			pot
			sink
			sofa
			stove
			toilet
			table
				There is ~.
				There are ~.
				
				Reading

Review 3

Unit 7 I Want to Play Outside

Structures	Vocabulary		Grammar

• What do you want to do?
  I want to play outside.
• What does she want to do?
  She wants to watch movies.
	buy new clothes
	catch fireflies
	climb the mountain
	cook food
	go to the sea
	listen to music
		play outside
		play music
		play the piano
		read comic books
		ride a scooter
		travel to Paris
			don't want to
			want to
			
			Reading

Unit 8 What Do You Want to Be?

Structures	Vocabulary		Grammar

• What do you want to be?
  I want to be a vet.
  I want to help animals.
•What does she want to be?
  She wants to be a designer.
• She wants to make clothes.
• I like to watch movies.
	designer
	movie director
	photographer
	pilot
	teacher
	traveler
	vet
	writer
		design clothes
		make movies
		take great pictures
		fly planes
		teach children
		travel around the world
		help animals
		write stories
			want to be
			want to
			
			Reading

Review 4

🎧 Midterm TEST 4C

107

Institute

Name

Score   /100

[1-2] Listen and choose.

1 ⓐ    ⓑ

ⓒ    ⓓ

2 ⓐ    ⓑ

ⓒ    ⓓ

[3-4] Listen and choose.

3    ⓐ   ⓑ   ⓒ   ⓓ

4    ⓐ   ⓑ   ⓒ   ⓓ

[5-6] Listen and choose.

5

ⓐ   ⓑ   ⓒ   ⓓ

6

ⓐ   ⓑ   ⓒ   ⓓ

7 Listen and choose.

ⓐ The jeans look cool.
ⓑ The puzzle looks interesting.
ⓒ The quiz looks difficult.
ⓓ The mask looks scary.

[8-9] Listen and mark O or X.

8

(   )

9

(   )

10 Listen and choose.

ⓐ    ⓑ

ⓒ 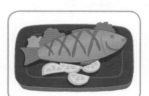   ⓓ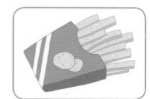

[11-12] Look and choose.

11

ⓐ I flew a drone.
ⓑ I saw a parade.
ⓒ I swam at the beach.
ⓓ I went to the water park.

12

ⓐ The lemonade is sour.
ⓑ The fruits are fresh.
ⓒ The pancakes are sweet.
ⓓ The ice cream is sour.

[13-14] Read and choose.

13

A: _____
B: Yes, please.

ⓐ What did you do?
ⓑ How's your salad?
ⓒ Can I try them on?
ⓓ May I take your order?

14

A: What size do you want?
B: _____

ⓐ I want red.   ⓑ It looks sweet.
ⓒ I want a small.   ⓓ I want new gloves.

15 Unscramble.

What _____?
(did / during / do / you / the vacation)

16 Read and write.

A: Look _____ this dress.
B: It _____ beautiful.

17 Read and choose.

A: How much are the jeans?
B: They're eighteen dollars.

ⓐ  ⓑ

ⓒ  ⓓ

18 Put the sentences in the order.

ⓐ It's spicy, but it's delicious.
ⓑ No, thanks. I'm full.
ⓒ How's the fried rice?
ⓓ Do you want some more?

(   ) → (   ) → (   ) → (   )

[19-20] Look and write.

19

A: May I take your order?
B: Yes, please. _____

20

A: What did you do last weekend?
B: I _____.

Final TEST 4C

Institute	
Name	
Score	/100

[1-2] Listen and choose.

1 　ⓐ　　ⓑ　　ⓒ　　ⓓ

2 　ⓐ　　ⓑ　　ⓒ　　ⓓ

3 Listen and choose.

ⓐ 　　ⓑ

ⓒ 　　ⓓ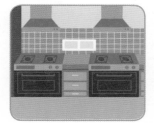

4 Listen and choose.

　ⓐ　　ⓑ　　ⓒ　　ⓓ

[5-6] Listen and choose.

5 ⓐ　　　ⓑ　　　ⓒ　　　ⓓ

6 ⓐ　　　ⓑ　　　ⓒ　　　ⓓ

[7-8] Listen and choose.

7 ⓐ 　　ⓑ

ⓒ 　　ⓓ

8 ⓐ 　　ⓑ

ⓒ 　　ⓓ

9 Listen and mark O or X.

(　　　　)

10 Listen and choose.

ⓐ　　　ⓑ　　　ⓒ　　　ⓓ

11 Read and choose.

> I want to be a _____.
> I want to help animals.

ⓐ teacher   ⓑ vet   ⓒ pilot   ⓓ designer

12 Read and choose.

ⓐ Do you want some water?
ⓑ Did you take a shower?
ⓒ Did you water the plants?
ⓓ Did you plant the flowers?

[13-14] Read and write the letter.

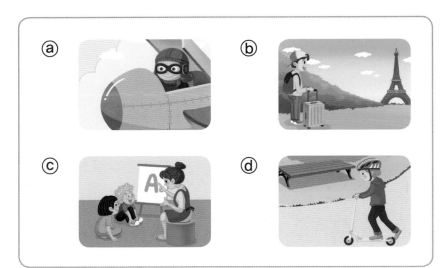

ⓐ   ⓑ
ⓒ   ⓓ

13

> A: What do you want to be?
> B: I want to be a pilot.

(   )

14

> A: What do you want to do?
> B: I want to travel to Paris.

(   )

15 Read and write.

> A: What's _____ the living room?
> B: _____ _____ two bookcases.

16 Unscramble.

> _____?
> (you / do / Did / homework / your)

17 Read and choose.

> I want to be a movie director.
> _____

ⓐ I want to design clothes.
ⓑ I want to write stories.
ⓒ I want to teach children.
ⓓ I want to make movies.

18 Look and choose.

ⓐ There is a bookcase in the bedroom.
ⓑ There is a closet in the bedroom.
ⓒ There are pictures on the wall.
ⓓ There are some toys in the box.

[19-20] Look and write.

19

> He wants to be a traveler.
> He wants _____.

20

> A: Did you _____?
> B: No, I didn't.

2nd Edition

LET'S GO

4c

to the English World

Word Book
& Workbook

CHUNJAE EDUCATION, INC.

Word Book

I'd Like a Chocolate Ice Cream Cone

Ⓐ Listen and repeat. 01 02

beef steak 비프스테이크	**I'd like a** beef steak. 저는 비프스테이크로 주세요.
noodles 국수	**I'd like** noodles. 저는 국수로 주세요.
french fries 프렌치프라이[감자튀김]	**Do you want some** french fries**?** 프렌치프라이를 좀 먹을래?
pancake 팬케이크	**Do you want some** pancakes**?** 팬케이크를 좀 먹을래?
sweet 단, 달콤한	**The ice cream is** sweet. 아이스크림은 달콤해.
sour (맛이) 신	**The lemonade is** sour. 레모네이드는 셔.
salty 짠	**The cheese pizza is** salty. 치즈피자는 짜.
spicy 매운	**The fried rice is** spicy. 볶음밥은 매워.

B Read, write, and say.

1 beef steak
비프스테이크

2 noodles
국수

3 french fries
프렌치프라이[감자튀김]

4 pancake
팬케이크

5 sweet
단, 달콤한

6 sour
(맛이) 신

7 salty
짠

8 spicy
매운

Learn More

order 주문	May I take your order? 주문하시겠어요?
some more 조금 더	Do you want some more? 좀 더 먹을래?
fresh 신선한	The salad is fresh. 샐러드는 신선해.
delicious 맛있는	It's delicious. 그것은 맛있어.

These Glasses Look Funny

A Listen and repeat.

interesting 재미있는, 흥미로운	**This book looks** interesting. 이 책은 재미있어 보여.
cool 멋진	**These jeans look** cool. 이 청바지는 멋져 보여.
beautiful 아름다운	**This dress looks** beautiful. 이 원피스는 아름다워 보여.
funny 우스운, 웃기는	**These glasses look** funny. 이 안경은 웃겨 보여.
scary 무서운	**That mask looks** scary. 저 가면은 무서워 보여.
difficult 어려운	**That quiz looks** difficult. 저 퀴즈는 어려워 보여.
easy 쉬운	**That puzzle looks** easy. 저 퍼즐은 쉬워 보여.
fresh 신선한	**These fruits look** fresh. 이 과일들은 신선해 보여.

B Read, write, and say.

1 interesting
재미있는, 흥미로운

_____ _____ _____ _____

2 cool
멋진

_____ _____ _____ _____

3 beautiful
아름다운

_____ _____ _____ _____

4 funny
우스운, 웃기는

_____ _____ _____ _____

5 scary
무서운

_____ _____ _____ _____

6 difficult
어려운

_____ _____ _____ _____

7 easy
쉬운

_____ _____ _____ _____

8 fresh
신선한

_____ _____ _____ _____

Learn More

buy 사다	May I buy these glasses? 이 안경을 사도 되나요?
look at ~을 보다	Look at this shirt. 이 셔츠 좀 봐.
look ~해 보이다	They look cute. 그것들은 귀여워 보여.

How much is it? 그것은 얼마예요? / **How much are they?** 그것들은 얼마예요?

How Much Are the Jeans?

A Listen and repeat. 🎧27 🎧28

sunglasses 선글라스	**How much are the sunglasses?** 그 선글라스는 얼마예요?
jeans 청바지	**How much are the jeans?** 그 청바지는 얼마예요?
gloves 장갑 (한 켤레)	**How much are the gloves?** 그 장갑은 얼마예요?
sneakers 운동화[스니커즈] (한 켤레)	**The sneakers are 13 dollars.** 그 운동화는 13달러예요.
rain boots 레인 부츠 (한 켤레)	**The rain boots are 20 dollars.** 그 레인 부츠는 20달러예요.
small 작은 크기	**I want a small, please.** 저는 작은 크기를 원해요.
medium 중간 크기	**I want a medium, please.** 저는 중간 크기를 원해요.
large 큰 크기	**I want a large, please.** 저는 큰 크기를 원해요.

1 sunglasses
선글라스

2 jeans
청바지

3 gloves
장갑 (한 켤레)

4 sneakers
운동화[스니커즈] (한 켤레)

5 rain boots
레인 부츠 (한 켤레)

6 small
작은 크기

7 medium
중간 크기

8 large
큰 크기

Learn More

size 크기, 사이즈	**What** size **do you want?** 어떤 크기를 원하세요?
color 색깔	**What** color **do you want?** 어떤 색깔을 원하세요?
try ~ on 입어[신어] 보다	**Can I** try them **on?** 그것들을 입어 봐도 되나요?
on sale 세일[할인 판매] 중인	**The shoes are** on sale. 신발은 할인 판매 중이에요.

I Went to the Water Park

A Listen and repeat. 40 41

went camping 캠핑하러 갔다	I went camping during the vacation. 나는 방학 동안에 캠핑하러 갔어.
went to the water park 워터파크에 갔다	I went to the water park yesterday. 나는 어제 워터파크에 갔어.
read many books 많은 책을 읽었다	I read many books during the vacation. 나는 방학 동안에 많은 책을 읽었어.
swam at the beach 해변에서 수영을 했다	She swam at the beach. 그녀는 해변에서 수영을 했어.
made a model plane 모형 비행기를 만들었다	He made a model plane last weekend. 그는 지난 주말에 모형 비행기를 만들었어.
ate Mexican food 멕시코 음식을 먹었다	We ate Mexican food. 우리는 멕시코 음식을 먹었어.
saw a parade 퍼레이드를 봤다	They saw a parade. 그들은 퍼레이드를 봤어.
flew a drone 드론을 날렸다	I flew a drone at the park. 나는 공원에서 드론을 날렸어.

1 went camping
캠핑하러 갔다

_____ _____ _____

2 went to the water park
워터파크에 갔다

_____ _____ _____

3 read many books
많은 책을 읽었다

_____ _____ _____

4 swam at the beach
해변에서 수영을 했다

_____ _____ _____

5 made a model plane
모형 비행기를 만들었다

_____ _____ _____

6 ate Mexican food
멕시코 음식을 먹었다

_____ _____ _____

7 saw a parade
퍼레이드를 봤다

_____ _____ _____

8 flew a drone
드론을 날렸다

_____ _____ _____

Learn More

during the vacation 방학 동안에	**What did you do** during the vacation**?** 너는 방학 동안에 무엇을 했니?
last weekend 지난 주말에	**We had a picnic** last weekend**.** 우리는 지난 주말에 소풍을 갔어.
yesterday 어제	**I rode a bike** yesterday**.** 나는 어제 자전거를 탔어.

A Listen and repeat. 53 54

take pictures 사진을 찍다	**Did you** take pictures**?** 너는 사진을 찍었니?
have lunch 점심을 먹다	**Did you** have lunch**?** 너는 점심을 먹었니?
see dolphins 돌고래들을 보다	**Did you** see dolphins**?** 너는 돌고래들을 봤니?
take a shower 샤워를 하다	**Did you** take a shower**?** 너는 샤워를 했니?
get a haircut 머리를 자르다	**Did she** get a haircut**?** 그녀는 머리를 잘랐니?
buy the tickets 표를 사다	**Did he** buy the tickets**?** 그는 표를 샀니?
water the plants 식물에 물을 주다	**Did they** water the plants**?** 그들은 식물에 물을 주었니?
bring your swimsuit 네 수영복을 가져오다	**Did you** bring your swimsuit**?** 너는 네 수영복을 가져왔니?
do your homework 네 숙제를 하다	**Did you** do your homework**?** 너는 네 숙제를 했니?

1 take pictures
사진을 찍다

2 have lunch
점심을 먹다

3 see dolphins
돌고래들을 보다

4 take a shower
샤워를 하다

5 get a haircut
머리를 자르다

6 buy the tickets
표를 사다

7 water the plants
식물에 물을 주다

8 bring your swimsuit
네 수영복을 가져오다

9 do your homework
네 숙제를 하다

Learn More

fantastic 아주 좋은, 환상적인	**It was** fantastic. 그것은 환상적이었어.
circus 서커스	**I went to the** circus. 나는 서커스에 갔어.

There Is a Nice Bed

A **Listen and repeat.** 66 67

bed 침대	**There is a** bed **in the bedroom.** 침실에 침대 한 개가 있어.
closet 옷장	**There are two** closets **in the bedroom.** 침실에 옷장 두 개가 있어.
bathtub 욕조	**There is a** bathtub **in the bathroom.** 욕실에 욕조 한 개가 있어.
toilet 변기	**There are two** toilets **in the bathroom.** 욕실에 변기 두 개가 있어.
sofa 소파	**There is a** sofa **in the living room.** 거실에 소파 한 개가 있어.
bookcase 책장	**There are two** bookcases **in the living room.** 거실에 책장 두 개가 있어.
stove 가스레인지	**There is a** stove **in the kitchen.** 부엌에 가스레인지 한 개가 있어.
sink 싱크대	**There are two** sinks **in the kitchen.** 부엌에 싱크대 두 개가 있어.

1 bed
침대

_____ _____ _____ _____

2 closet
옷장

_____ _____ _____ _____

3 bathtub
욕조

_____ _____ _____ _____

4 toilet
변기

_____ _____ _____ _____

5 sofa
소파

_____ _____ _____ _____

6 bookcase
책장

_____ _____ _____ _____

7 stove
가스레인지

_____ _____ _____ _____

8 sink
싱크대

_____ _____ _____ _____

Learn More

bedroom 침실   **living room** 거실   **kitchen** 부엌   **bathroom** 욕실

on the wall 벽에 | **There are pictures** on the wall. 벽에 그림들이 있어.

I Want to Play Outside

Ⓐ Listen and repeat. 🎧79 🎧80

travel to Paris 파리로 여행하다	**I want to** travel to Paris. 나는 파리로 여행하고 싶어.
go to the sea 바다에 가다	**I want to** go to the sea. 나는 바다에 가고 싶어.
climb the mountain 등산하다	**I want to** climb the mountain. 나는 등산하고 싶어.
catch fireflies 반딧불이들을 잡다	**She wants to** catch fireflies. 그녀는 반딧불이들을 잡고 싶어 해.
buy new clothes 새 옷을 사다	**He wants to** buy new clothes. 그는 새 옷을 사고 싶어 해.
read comic books 만화책을 읽다	**They want to** read comic books. 그들은 만화책을 읽고 싶어 해.
listen to music 음악을 듣다	**I don't want to** listen to music. 나는 음악을 듣고 싶지 않아.
ride a scooter 스쿠터를 타다	**I don't like to** ride a scooter. 나는 스쿠터 타는 것을 좋아하지 않아.

1 travel to Paris
파리로 여행하다

_____ _____ _____

2 go to the sea
바다에 가다

_____ _____ _____

3 climb the mountain
등산하다

_____ _____ _____

4 catch fireflies
반딧불이들을 잡다

_____ _____ _____

5 buy new clothes
새 옷을 사다

_____ _____ _____

6 read comic books
만화책을 읽다

_____ _____ _____

7 listen to music
음악을 듣다

_____ _____ _____

8 ride a scooter
스쿠터를 타다

_____ _____ _____

Learn More

bored 지루한	**I'm so** bored. 나는 정말 지루해.
play outside 밖에서 놀다	**I want to** play outside. 나는 밖에서 놀고 싶어.
play music 음악을 연주하다	**My friends and I will** play music. 내 친구들과 나는 음악을 연주할 거야.

What Do You Want to Be?

Listen and repeat. 92 93

designer 디자이너	**I want to be a** designer. 나는 디자이너가 되고 싶어.
movie director 영화감독	**I want to be a** movie director. 나는 영화감독이 되고 싶어.
photographer 사진작가	**I want to be a** photographer. 나는 사진작가가 되고 싶어.
traveler 여행가	**I want to be a** traveler. 나는 여행가가 되고 싶어.
design clothes 옷을 디자인하다	**I want to** design clothes. 나는 옷을 디자인하고 싶어.
write stories 이야기를 쓰다	**I want to** write stories. 나는 이야기를 쓰고 싶어.
teach children 아이들을 가르치다	**She wants to** teach children. 그녀는 아이들을 가르치고 싶어 해.
make movies 영화를 만들다	**He wants to** make movies. 그는 영화를 만들고 싶어 해.
help animals 동물들을 돕다	**I want to** help animals. 나는 동물들을 돕고 싶어.
fly planes 비행기를 조종하다	**He wants to** fly planes. 그는 비행기를 조종하고 싶어 해.
take great pictures 멋진 사진을 찍다	**I want to** take great pictures. 나는 멋진 사진을 찍고 싶어.
travel around the world 전 세계를 여행하다, 세계 일주를 하다	**I want to** travel around the world. 나는 전 세계를 여행하고 싶어.

B Read, write, and say.

□ Read □ Write □ Say

1 designer
디자이너

2 movie director
영화감독

3 photographer
사진작가

4 traveler
여행가

5 design clothes
옷을 디자인하다

6 write stories
이야기를 쓰다

7 teach children
아이들을 가르치다

8 make movies
영화를 만들다

9 help animals
동물들을 돕다

10 fly planes
비행기를 조종하다

11 take great pictures
멋진 사진을 찍다

12 travel around the world
전 세계를 여행하다, 세계 일주를 하다

Learn More

singer 가수	writer 작가	teacher 선생님	vet 수의사
pilot 조종사, 비행사	cook 요리사	scientist 과학자	doctor 의사
police officer 경찰관	soccer player 축구 선수		

Workbook

I'd Like a Chocolate Ice Cream Cone

Words

Ⓐ Look and circle.

1

beef steak : cheese pizza

2

noodles : ice cream

3

fried rice : french fries

4

pancakes : lemonade

Ⓑ Look and match.

1

2

3

4

The ice cream is • • salty.

The lemonade is • • spicy.

The fried rice is • • sweet.

The pizza is • • sour.

Practice

(A) Read and match.

1

A: May I take your order?
B: Yes, please. I'd like pancakes.

ⓐ

2

A: May I take your order?
B: Yes, please. I'd like noodles.

ⓑ

3

A: May I take your order?
B: Yes, please. I'd like a beef steak.

ⓒ

(B) Write and check.

ice cream   fried rice   lemonade   cheese pizza

1

How's your _____?

☐ It's sour.   ☐ It's salty.

2

How's your _____?

☐ It's spicy.   ☐ It's sweet.

3

How's your _____?

☐ It's spicy.   ☐ It's sour.

4

How's your _____?

☐ It's salty.   ☐ It's sweet.

Write & Talk

A Write and circle.

1

A: _____ _____ take your order?

B: Yes, please. I'd like (french fries / pancakes).

2

A: May I _____ _____ _____?

B: Yes, please. I'd like (a beef steak / noodles).

3

A: _____ your lemonade?

B: It's (salty / sour).

4

A: _____ your fried rice?

B: It's (sweet / spicy).

B Read and write.

> ⓐ I'd like pancakes. ⓑ Do you want some more?
>
> ⓒ How's the fried rice? ⓓ Yes, please.

1

A: _____

B: It's spicy, but it's delicious.

A: _____

B: No, thanks. I'm full.

2

A: May I take your order?

B: Yes, please. _____

A: Do you want some juice, too?

B: _____

Reading

A Read and circle T or F.

Crepes are my favorite dessert.
They are pancakes from France.
I like fruit crepes.
They are sweet and fresh.

Gelato is ice cream from Italy.
Lemon gelato is my favorite.
It is sweet and sour. It is delicious!
Try some. You will like it.

1   Crepes are cupcakes from Italy.   (T / F)

2   Fruit crepes are sweet and fresh.   (T / F)

3   Gelato is ice cream from Italy.   (T / F)

4   Lemon gelato is sweet and spicy.   (T / F)

B Read and write.

1

A: May I take your order?

B: Yes, please. _____

2

A: _____

B: It's sour.

3

A: How's your chicken?

B: _____

Build Up

Ⓐ Unscramble and match.

1

A: Do _____?
          (you / some / want / juice)

B: Yes, please.

ⓐ

2

A: Do _____?
          (some / cookies / you / want)

B: No, thanks.

ⓑ

3

A: Do _____?
          (want / grapes / some / you)

B: No, thanks.

ⓒ

4

A: Do _____?
          (more / some / want / you / bread)

B: Yes, please. It's delicious.

ⓓ

5

A: Do _____?
          (sandwiches / some / want / more / you)

B: No, thanks. I'm full.

ⓔ

A Make the sentence.

1 _____

(I / take / order / your / May / ?) 주문하시겠어요?

2 _____

(like / I'd / a beef steak / .) 저는 비프스테이크로 주세요.

3 _____

(I'd / pancakes / like / .) 저는 팬케이크로 주세요.

4 _____

(How's / ice cream / your / ?) 네 아이스크림은 어때?

5 _____

(and / It's / sour / sweet / .) 그것은 새콤달콤해.

6 _____

(some / Do / want / you / noodles / ?) 국수를 좀 먹을래?

7 _____

(Do / some / you / want / water / ?) 물 좀 마실래?

These Glasses Look Funny

Words

A Look and write the letter.

ⓐ interesting　　ⓑ funny　　ⓒ easy　　ⓓ fresh　　ⓔ difficult　　ⓕ beautiful

1

2

3

4

5

6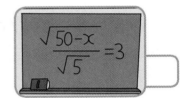

B Circle and write.

1

The mask looks _____.

(fresh / scary)

2

The jeans look _____.

(cool / easy)

3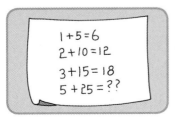

The quiz looks _____.

(funny / easy)

Practice

A Read and match.

1 Look at these glasses. • •  • • It looks easy.

2 Look at this mask. • •  • • They look funny.

3 Look at this puzzle. • •  • • It looks scary.

B Look and choose.

1

Look at this quiz.
ⓐ It looks scary.
ⓑ It looks difficult.

2

Look at this book.
ⓐ It looks interesting.
ⓑ It looks fresh.

3

Look at these fruits.
ⓐ They look easy.
ⓑ They look fresh.

4

Look at these flowers.
ⓐ They look funny.
ⓑ They look beautiful.

Write & Talk

Ⓐ Circle and write.

1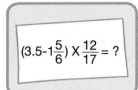

A: Look at (this / these) _____.

B: It looks _____.

2

A: Look at (this / these) _____.

B: It _____ _____.

3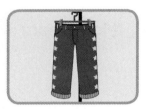

A: Look at (this / these) _____.

B: They _____ _____.

4

A: Look at (this / these) _____.

B: They _____ _____.

jeans
book
glasses
quiz

difficult
cool
funny
interesting

Ⓑ Read and write.

A: Look at this shirt. **1** _____

B: I don't like yellow.

A: **2** _____

B: It looks cool. I like it.

A: **3** _____

C: It's twenty dollars.

ⓐ How much is it?

ⓑ It looks cute.

ⓒ How about this T-shirt?

Reading

(A) Read and match.

1

Terry is sleeping in his bed.
He looks cute.

(a)

2

Some soup and bread are on the table.
They look delicious.

(b)

3

Some fruits are in the basket.
They look fresh.

(c)

(B) Read and write.

| They look cool. | They look cute. | It looks beautiful. |

1

A: Look at this picture.

B: _____

2

A: Look at those jackets.

B: _____

3

A: Look at these dolls.

B: _____

Build Up

Ⓐ Read and circle.

1 The cap (look / looks) cool.

2 The girl (look / looks) happy.

3 These vegetables (look / looks) fresh.

4 These glasses (look / looks) funny.

Ⓑ Make the sentence.

The man / funny ····▸ The man looks funny.

1 These birds / beautiful

····▸ _____

2 The cupcakes / delicious

····▸ _____

3 The boy / sleepy

····▸ _____

4 The game / interesting

····▸ _____

 **Writing**

(A) Make the sentence.

1 _____

(at / dress / this / Look / .) 이 원피스를 봐.

2 _____

(these / at / glasses / Look / .) 이 안경을 봐.

3 _____

(looks / It / funny / .) 그것은 우스워 보여.

4 _____

(looks / He / cute / .) 그는 귀여워 보여.

5 _____

(interesting / look / They / .) 그것들은 재미있어 보여.

6 _____

(This / fresh / fruit salad / looks / .) 이 과일 샐러드는 신선해 보여.

7 _____

(cool / jeans / look / These / .) 이 청바지는 멋져 보여.

How Much Are the Jeans?

Words

A Look and write.

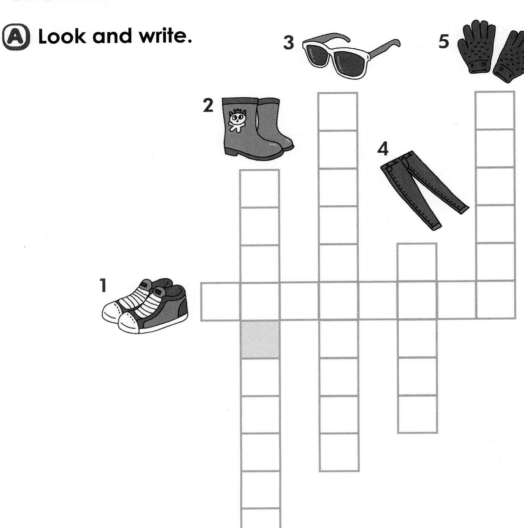

jeans

gloves

sunglasses

sneakers

rain boots

B Look and write.

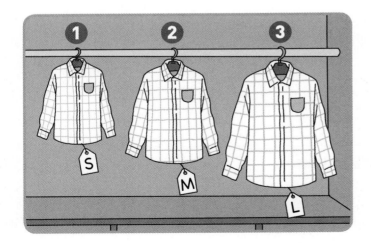

1   I want a _____, please.

2   I want a _____, please.

3   I want a _____, please.

medium   small   large

Practice

Ⓐ Read and match.

1

A: How much are the sunglasses?

B: They're ten dollars.

ⓐ $25

2

A: How much are the gloves?

B: They're seven dollars.

ⓑ $10

3

A: How much are the rain boots?

B: They're twenty five dollars.

ⓒ $7

4

A: How much are the sneakers?

B: They're thirty dollars.

ⓓ $30

Ⓑ Write and check.

1

_____ do you want?

☐ I want a small, please. ☐ I want a medium, please.

2

_____ do you want?

☐ I want a large, please. ☐ I want a medium, please.

3

_____ do you want?

☐ I want a large, please. ☐ I want a small, please.

Write & Talk

A Write and circle.

1

A: _____ are the rain boots?

B: They're (thirty dollars / twenty dollars).

2

A: _____ do you want?

B: I want a (small / medium), please.

3

A: _____ do you want?

B: I want (blue / red).

B Read and write.

A: I'm looking for gloves.

B: **1** _____

A: I want blue, please.

B: **2** _____

A: They look nice.

3 _____

B: Sure.

ⓐ How about these?

ⓑ Can I try them on?

ⓒ What color do you want?

Reading

Ⓐ Read and write.

I want those _____.

They are red and white.

They look _____.

_____ are they?

They're twenty two dollars.

But I have only twenty in my _____.

Oh, they're _____. They're twenty dollars.

Shoe Store

$20 SALE

| How much | sneakers | on sale | cool | wallet |

Ⓑ Read and write.

1

$18

How much are the jeans?

···▸ They _____.

2

B   L

What size do you want?

···▸ I _____.

3

녹색

What color do you want?

···▸ I _____.

Build Up

Ⓐ Write and match.

color　animal　subject　size　dessert

1

A: _____ do you want?

B: I _____ a medium, please.

ⓐ

2

A: _____ do you want?

B: I _____ purple, please.

ⓑ

3

A: _____ do you like?

B: I _____ P.E.

ⓒ

4

A: _____ do you want?

B: I _____ pancakes.

ⓓ

5

A: _____ do you like?

B: I _____ dogs.

ⓔ

Writing

A Make the sentence.

1 _____

(are / the sunglasses / How much / ?) 그 선글라스는 얼마예요?

2 _____

(want / you / do / What size / ?) 당신은 어떤 크기를 원하세요?

3 _____

(you / want / What color / do / ?) 당신은 어떤 색깔을 원하세요?

4 _____

(fifteen / The sneakers / are / dollars / .) 그 운동화는 15달러예요.

5 _____

(want / a large. / I / please / .) 저는 큰 크기를 원해요.

6 _____

(I'm / gloves / looking for / .) 저는 장갑을 찾고 있어요.

7 _____

(them / try / I / on / Can / ?) 그것들을 입어 봐도 되나요?

I Went to the Water Park

Words

Ⓐ Look and match.

1

went • • at the beach

2

swam • • a model plane

3

read • • to the water park

4

made • • many books

Ⓑ Look and write.

1

I _____.

2

I _____.

3

I _____.

4

I _____.

flew a drone

went camping

ate Mexican food

saw a parade

Practice

Ⓐ Look and write T or F.

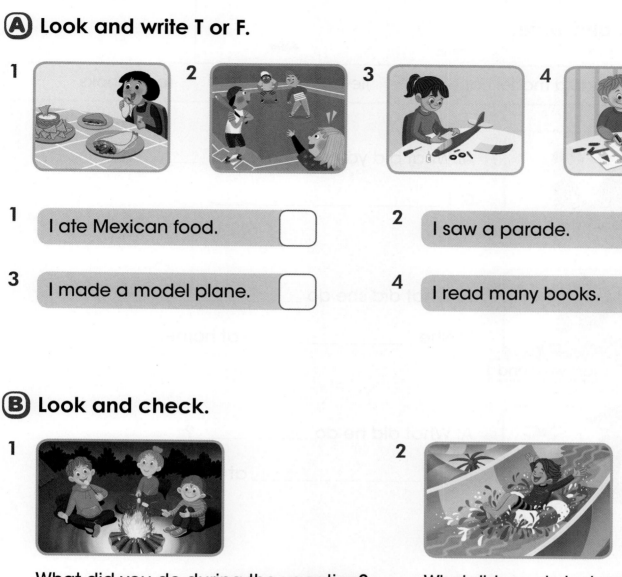

1
I ate Mexican food. ☐

2
I saw a parade. ☐

3
I made a model plane. ☐

4
I read many books. ☐

Ⓑ Look and check.

1

What did you do during the vacation?
- ☐ I went camping.
- ☐ I read many books.

2

What did you do last weekend?
- ☐ I ate delicious food.
- ☐ I went to the water park.

3

What did you do during the vacation?
- ☐ I saw a parade.
- ☐ I read many books.

4

What did you do last weekend?
- ☐ I made a model plane.
- ☐ I flew a drone.

Write & Talk

A Look and write.

made a model car	flew a drone	read books

1

vacation

A: What did you do during the _____?

B: I _____.

2

last weekend

A: What did she do _____?

B: She _____ at home.

3

yesterday

A: What did he do _____?

B: He _____ at the park.

B Write and number in order.

2   I _____ to the zoo.

☐   What did you do _____?

4   I _____ an animal parade.

☐   What did you _____ there?

☐   I _____ a bird show, too.

☐   Sounds fun.

saw

see

went

yesterday

watched

40

Reading

A Read and circle T or F.

Brian went to the beach last weekend.

He went there with Tim.

They played together.

They swam at the beach.

They made a sand castle, too.

Lunch was delicious.

They ate hot dogs and french fries.

1 Brian went to the water park with Tim.   (T / F)

2 They swam at the beach.   (T / F)

3 They made a sand castle.   (T / F)

4 They ate hamburgers for lunch.   (T / F)

B Read and match.

1
> A: What did you do during the vacation?
> B: I went to the water park. It was fun.

ⓐ

2
> A: What did she do last weekend?
> B: She went camping with her family.

ⓑ

3
> He went to the food festival.
> He ate Mexican food there.

ⓒ

Build Up

A Change and write.

1 make — made

2 see —

3 eat —

4 ride —

5 swim —

6 draw —

7 read —

8 have —

B Correct and rewrite.

1

I <u>have</u> a fun time last weekend.

···▶ _____

2

He <u>draws</u> many pictures during the vacation.

···▶ _____

3

She <u>makes</u> a robot last weekend.

···▶ _____

4

We <u>fly</u> kites yesterday.

···▶ _____

Writing

Ⓐ Make the sentence.

1 _____

(the vacation / during / What / do / you / did / ?) 너는 방학 동안에 무엇을 했니?

2 _____

(did / What / you / last weekend / do / ?) 너는 지난 주말에 무엇을 했니?

3 _____

(did / What / see / you / there / ?) 너는 거기서 무엇을 봤니?

4 _____

(camping / I / last weekend / went / .) 나는 지난 주말에 캠핑을 갔어.

5 _____

(many books / during / read / the vacation / She / .) 그녀는 방학 동안에 많은 책을 읽었어.

6 _____

(at the beach / He / last weekend / swam / .) 그는 지난 주말에 해변에서 수영했어.

7 _____

(a / time / We / great / had / .) 우리는 아주 멋진 시간을 보냈어.

Did You Take Pictures?

Words

A Look and write the letter.

ⓐ see dolphins	ⓑ buy the tickets	ⓒ do your homework
ⓓ get a haircut	ⓔ take a shower	ⓕ bring your swimsuit

1

2

3

4

5

6

B Circle and write.

1

Did you _____?

(water the plants / take a shower)

2

Did you _____?

(get a haircut / have lunch)

3

Did you _____?

(bring your swimsuit / bring your umbrella)

Practice

A Look and choose.

1

ⓐ Did you buy the tickets?

ⓑ Did you borrow books?

2

ⓐ Did you water the plants?

ⓑ Did you plant the flowers?

3

ⓐ Did you buy new shoes?

ⓑ Did you bring your swimsuit?

4

ⓐ Did you take a shower?

ⓑ Did you have lunch?

B Read and write the letter. Then check.

ⓐ  ⓑ  ⓒ  ⓓ

1

Did you do your homework? ☐

☐ Yes, I did. ☐ No, I didn't.

2

Did you have lunch? ☐

☐ Yes, I did. ☐ No, I didn't.

3

Did you get a haircut? ☐

☐ Yes, I did. ☐ No, I didn't.

4

Did you see dolphins? ☐

☐ Yes, I did. ☐ No, I didn't.

Write & Talk

A Look and write.

1

A: Did you _____ today?

B: Yes, _____ .

2

A: Did you _____?

B: No, _____ .

3

A: Did you _____ today?

B: Yes, _____ .

4

A: Did you _____?

B: No, _____ .

buy the tickets   water the plants   take a shower   have breakfast

B Read and write.

A: You look nice.

1 _____

B: Yes, I did. **2** _____

A: It was good. I visited the Sea Park.

B: **3** _____

A: Yes, I did. I played with the dolphins.

ⓐ Did you see dolphins there?

ⓑ Did you get a haircut today?

ⓒ How was your day?

Reading

Ⓐ Read and write.

_____ have a good day?

I had a _____.

I went to the _____.

I _____ a big elephant there.

He _____ with a big ball.

I saw a cute bear, too.

She _____ a bike very well.

The show was _____.

| Did you | played | circus | fantastic | rode | great day | saw |

Ⓑ Read and write.

1

I went to the zoo today.
I saw my favorite animal.

Tony

A: Did Tony go to the zoo?

B: _____

A: What did he see there?

B: He _____.

2

I went to the river today.
I swam in the river.

Ann

A: Ann _____ today.

B: Did she catch fish there?

A: _____

She _____.

Build Up

A Write and match.

| have | clean | make | fly | swim | water |

1

A: _____ a model plane?

B: Yes, I did.

ⓐ

2

A: _____ at the beach?

B: No, he didn't.

ⓑ

3

A: _____ lunch?

B: Yes, she did.

ⓒ

4

A: _____ his room?

B: No, he didn't.

ⓓ

5

A: _____ a kite?

B: Yes, I did.

ⓔ

6

A: _____ the plants?

B: No, she didn't.

ⓕ

Ⓐ Make the sentence.

1 _____

(you / Did / a haircut / get / ?) 너는 머리를 잘랐니?

2 _____

(bring / you / your swimsuit / Did / ?) 너는 네 수영복을 가져왔니?

3 _____

(he / the tickets / Did / buy / ?) 그는 표를 샀니?

4 _____

(Did / see / there / dolphins / you / ?) 너는 거기서 돌고래들을 봤니?

5 _____

(homework / do / Did / she / her / ?) 그녀는 숙제를 했니?

6 _____

(you / have / day / a good / Did / ?) 너는 좋은 하루를 보냈니?

7 _____

(rode / She / very well / a bike / .) 그녀는 자전거를 아주 잘 탔어.

There Is a Nice Bed

Words

A Look and write.

| bed | stove | toilet | sofa | closet | bathtub |

1

_____

2

_____

3

_____

4

_____

5

_____

6

_____

B Circle and write.

1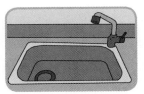

There is _____.
(a stove / a sink)

2

There are _____.
(two sofas / two beds)

3

There are _____.
(two closets / two bookcases)

Practice

A Write and match.

1   There _____ a bookcase.   •

2   There _____ two beds.   •

3   There _____ two stoves.   •

ⓐ   •

ⓑ   •

ⓒ   •

B Look and check.

1
What's in the bedroom?
☐ There is a bed.
☐ There are two closets.

2
What's in the living room?
☐ There is a sofa.
☐ There is a table.

3
What's in the kitchen?
☐ There are two sinks.
☐ There are two stoves.

4
What's in the bathroom?
☐ There are two toilets.
☐ There is a bathtub.

Write & Talk

Ⓐ Look and write.

1

A: What's in the _____?

B: There _____ a _____.

2

A: What's in the _____?

B: _____ a _____.

3

A: What's in the _____?

B: There _____ two _____.

4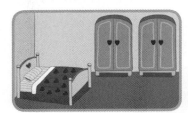

A: What's in the _____?

B: _____ two _____.

bedroom
living room
kitchen
bathroom
closets
table
toilets
sink

Ⓑ Read and write T or F.

1 There is a bookcase in the room. ☐

2 There are some toys in the box. ☐

3 There are pictures on the wall. ☐

4 There is a bed in the room. ☐

Reading

A Read and write.

My doll, Pamela has a new house.

It has a bedroom and a kitchen.

There is a sofa and a bed in the bedroom.

There is a table and a stove in the kitchen.

There are two chairs, too.

What is Pamela doing? She is making pancakes.

1   There is _____ and _____ in Pamela's house.

2   What's in the kitchen?   ···▸ There is _____ and _____ .

                               ···▸ There are _____ .

3   What is Pamela doing?   ···▸ She is _____ .

B Look and write.

1   There _____ in the bedroom.

    There is a closet, too.

    _____ in the closet.

2   _____ in the living room.

    There is a bookcase, too.

    _____ on the wall.

| a bed | two pictures | clothes | a sofa |

Build Up

Ⓐ Read and circle.

1   (There is / There are) a lamp next to the sofa.

2   (There is / There are) two cats on the sofa.

3   (There is / There are) a closet in the bedroom.

4   (There is / There are) a new bed in my room.

5   (There is / There are) many balls in the box.

Ⓑ Write and match.

1   _____ a piano next to the pot.   •

Ⓐ

2   _____ a toilet in the bathroom.   •

Ⓑ

3   _____ pictures on the wall.   •

Ⓒ

4   _____ bookcases in the living room.   •

Ⓓ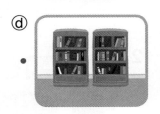

5   _____ some books on the desk.   •

Ⓔ

54

Ⓐ Make the sentence.

1 _____

(the kitchen / in / What's / ?) 부엌에는 무엇이 있니?

2 _____

(in / What's / the living room / ?) 거실에는 무엇이 있니?

3 _____

(the bathroom / is / in / a bathtub / There / .) 욕실에는 욕조 한 개가 있어.

4 _____

(in / a bookcase / is / the living room / There / .) 거실에는 책장 한 개가 있어.

5 _____

(beds / in the bedroom / There / two / are / .) 침실에는 침대 두 개가 있어.

6 _____

(two / on the wall / There / pictures / are / .) 벽에는 그림 두 개가 있어.

7 _____

(and a stove / in the kitchen / There / a table / is / .)
부엌에는 식탁 한 개와 가스레인지 한 개가 있어.

I Want to Play Outside

Words

Ⓐ Look and match.

1  •

2  •

3  •

4  •

• listen •

• ride •

• climb •

• read •

• the mountain

• to music

• comic books

• a scooter

Ⓑ Look and write.

1

I want to _____.

2

I want to _____.

buy new clothes

go to the sea

catch fireflies

travel to Paris

3

I want to _____.

4

I want to _____.

Practice

A Circle and write.

1
I want to (ride a scooter / catch fireflies).

....▶ _____

2
I want to (go to the sea / climb the mountain).

....▶ _____

3
I want to (read comic books / listen to music).

....▶ _____

B Read and write the letter.

ⓐ 　ⓑ 　ⓒ 　ⓓ

1
A: What do you want to do?
B: I want to read comic books.
☐

2
A: What do you want to do?
B: I want to buy new clothes.
☐

3
A: What do you want to do?
B: I want to travel to Paris.
☐

4
A: What do you want to do?
B: I want to climb the mountain.
☐

Write & Talk

A Look and write.

1    2    3    4

1 A: What do you _____ to do?

    B: I want to _____.

2 A: What _____ want to do?

    B: I want _____.

3 A: What does he _____ to do?

    B: He wants _____.

4 A: What _____ want to do?

    B: She wants _____.

> ride a scooter   travel to New York   watch movies   climb the mountain

B Read and number in order.

[1] What do you want to do today?

[ ] Okay. Then I'll cook for you.

[4] What do you want to eat?

[ ] I want to sleep. I'm tired. But I'm hungry.

[ ] Good. That's easy.

[ ] I want to eat spaghetti.

Reading

A Read and write.

The school concert is this Friday.

My friends and I will _____.

Sally wants _____ the piano.

Ron wants to play the guitar.

Tom _____ to play the drums.

"Kate, what will you do?"

I _____ play the piano or the guitar.

I _____ like to play the drums.

But I like _____.

I _____ to sing songs.

| to sing | to play | don't | can't | want | wants | play music |

B Read and match.

1

My birthday is tomorrow.
I want to have a big party.

ⓐ

2

Sam wants to play outside.
He wants to catch fireflies.

ⓑ

3

Anna likes to play music.
She wants to play the drums.

ⓒ

Build Up

Ⓐ Look and write.

1

I don't want _____.

I want _____.

2

I don't like _____.

I like _____.

3

I don't want _____.

I _____.

4

I don't like _____.

I _____.

5

I don't want _____.

I _____.

---

watch sports	visit the museum	ride a bike	stay home
ride a scooter	practice the piano	study math	play outside
play computer games		climb the mountain	

A Make the sentence.

1 _____

(you / What / do / to do / want / ?) 너는 무엇을 하고 싶니?

2 _____

(want / he / does / to do / What / ?) 그는 무엇을 하고 싶어 하니?

3 _____

(to read / I / want / comic books / .) 나는 만화책을 읽고 싶어.

4 _____

(wants / fireflies / He / to catch / .) 그는 반딧불이들을 잡고 싶어 해.

5 _____

(new clothes / to buy / wants / She / .) 그녀는 새 옷을 사고 싶어 해.

6 _____

(don't / I / like / the drums / to play / .) 나는 드럼 치는 것을 좋아하지 않아.

7 _____

(home / want / I / to stay / don't / .) 나는 집에 있고 싶지 않아.

What Do You Want to Be?

Words

(A) Look and write.

| fly planes | design clothes | help animals | write stories |

1

_____

2

_____

3

_____

4

_____

(B) Look and circle.

1

I want to be a (designer / movie director).

I want to (make movies / design clothes).

2

I want to be a (photographer / writer).

I want to (write stories / take great pictures).

3

I want to be a (traveler / pilot).

I want to (fly planes / travel around the world).

4

I want to be a (vet / teacher).

I want to (teach children / help animals).

Practice

A Read and choose.

1

   ⓐ I want to be a teacher.

   ⓑ I want to be a photographer.

2

   ⓐ I want to make movies.

   ⓑ I want to travel around the world.

3

   ⓐ I want to be a vet. I want to help animals.

   ⓑ I want to be a doctor. I want to help people.

B Write and match.

> write stories   design clothes   fly planes

1

A: What do you want to be?

B: I want to _____ a pilot.

   I want to _____.

ⓐ

2

A: What do you want to be?

B: I want _____ a writer.

   I want _____.

ⓑ

3

A: What do you want to be?

B: I _____ a designer.

   I want _____.

ⓒ

Write & Talk

A Look and write.

1.

   A: What do you want to _____?

   B: I want to be _____.

     I want to _____.

2.

   A: What do you _____ be?

   B: I want to _____.

     I want _____.

3.

   A: What do you _____ be?

   B: I want to _____.

     I want _____.

4.

   A: What _____ you _____ be?

   B: I want _____.

     I want _____.

5.

   A: What _____ want _____?

   B: I want _____.

     I want _____.

| a writer   a teacher   a cook | teach English   fly planes   help people |
| a pilot   a police officer | write stories   make delicious food |

Reading

A Read and write.

Hello, my name is Alice.

I like to watch movies.

I want to be a movie director.

I want to make science movies.

I will join the movie festival this summer.

1   What does Alice like to do?   ···▸ She likes _____.

2   What does she want to be?   ···▸ She wants _____.

3   What does she want to do?   ···▸ She wants _____.

B Read and write T or F.

1    2    3    4

1
I like to sing songs.
I want to be a singer.
☐

2
My favorite subject is science.
I want to be a scientist.
☐

3
She wants to be a doctor.
She wants to help sick people.
☐

4
He likes to play soccer.
He wants to be a soccer player.
☐

Build Up

Ⓐ Make the sentence.

1

a writer / write stories

I want to be _____.

I want to _____.

2

scientists / make robots

They want to _____.

They want _____.

3

a photographer / take good pictures

He wants _____.

He wants _____.

4

a doctor / help sick people

She _____.

She _____.

5

a designer / design clothes

Mary _____.

She _____.

A Make the sentence.

1 _____

(you / What / to be / do / want / ?) 너는 무엇이 되고 싶니?

2 _____

(want / a photographer / I / to be / .) 나는 사진작가가 되고 싶어.

3 _____

(to be / He / a teacher / wants / .) 그는 선생님이 되고 싶어 해.

4 _____

(planes / wants / She / to fly / .) 그녀는 비행기를 조종하고 싶어 해.

5 _____

(delicious food / want / I / to make / .) 나는 맛있는 음식을 만들고 싶어.

6 _____

(She / to travel / around the world / wants / .) 그녀는 전 세계를 여행하고 싶어 해.

7 _____

(movies / wants / to / He / make / .) 그는 영화를 만들고 싶어 해.